* WE ARE AMERICA *

Korean Americans

TIFFANY PETERSON

Heinemann Library
Chicago, Illinois

© 2003 Heinemann Library
a division of Reed Elsevier Inc.
Chicago, Illinois

Customer Service 888-454-2279

Visit our website at www.heinemannlibrary.com

Created by the publishing team at Heinemann Library
Designed by Roslyn Broder
Photo research by Amor Montes de Oca
Printed and Bound in the United States by Lake Book Manufacturing, Inc.

07 06 05 04 03
10 9 8 7 6 5 4 3 2 1

Library of Congress Cataloging-in-Publication Data
Peterson, Tiffany.
    Korean Americans / Tiffany Peterson.
      p. cm. — (We are America)
    Summary: Briefly discusses some of the reasons that Koreans
have come to live in the United States, how they have preserved
Korean customs and traditions in their new homeland, and what
life is like for them here.
    Includes bibliographical references (p.) and index.
    ISBN 1-40340-735-5 (lib. bdg.) ISBN 1-40343-136-1 (pbk.)
    1. Korean Americans—Juvenile literature. 2. Immigrants—United States—Juvenile literature. 3. United States—Emigration and immigration—Juvenile literature. 4. Korea—Emigration and immigration—Juvenile literature. 5. Korean
Americans—Biography
  —Juvenile literature. 6. Immigrants—United States—Biography
  —Juvenile literature.   [1. Korean Americans. 2. United States
  —Emigration and immigration.]   I. Title. II. Series.
E184.K6P48 2003
973.04'957—dc21
                                                            2002013099

Acknowledgments
The author and publishers are grateful to the following for permission to reproduce copyright material:
pp. 4, 5, 28, 29 Courtesy of Dr. John Han; p. 6 Hulton Archive/Getty Images; pp. 8, 9, 10, 11, 12, 13, 14 Bishop Museum; pp. 15, 17 Helen Ahn Collection; p. 16 The Granger Collection; p. 19 Jose Luis Pelaez, Inc./Corbis; p. 20 AP Wide World Photos; p. 21 Myrleen Ferguson Cate/PhotoEdit, Inc.; p. 22 Tony Freeman/PhotoEdit, Inc.; p. 23 Robert Brenner/PhotoEdit, Inc.; p. 24 Gary Conner/PhotoEdit, Inc.; p. 25 Jim Whitmer; p. 26 Michael Newman/PhotoEdit, Inc.; p. 27 Cathy Melloan/PhotoEdit, Inc.

Cover photographs by (foreground) Robert Brenner/PhotoEdit, Inc., (background) David R. Frazier Photolibrary

Special thanks to Moo-Young Han, editor in chief of the Society of Korean-American Scholars, for his comments in preparation of this book, Younghee Hong, and Dr. John Han, for sharing his story.

Some words are shown in bold, **like this.** You can find out what they mean by looking in the glossary.

On the cover of this book, a Korean-American family is shown. A present-day photo of a Korean neighborhood in Los Angeles, California, is shown in the background.

Contents

Jongha Han's Story

Jongha Han wanted to be a doctor. He went to medical school at Seoul National University in South Korea. When it was time for his training, he decided to move to the United

Jongha added the American name John when he came to the U.S. His new name was Jongha John Han.

States. In 1967, Jongha, his wife, Ahcha, and their five-month-old daughter, Wonson, left South Korea for the United States. They had a long trip ahead of them.

The Hans are seen here outside the airport in Seoul, South Korea, on the day they left for the United States in 1967.

Jongha decided to leave Korea because there were few jobs and little money there. There were very few places in Korea where he could continue studying to become a doctor. Most of the students in Jongha's class came to the United States to finish their training. The Hans, like many Korean **immigrants,** planned to stay long enough for Jongha to finish his training. They hoped they would be able to save enough money to return to South Korea.

Many of the Koreans who moved to the United States about the same time the Hans did became highly successful. Here, the Hans are seen in Korea with their daughter, Wonson.

When we came to New York . . . people were very receiving and welcoming to us. Not only inside the hospital, but outside, in the neighborhood.
—Dr. Jongha John Han

Korea

Korea is located in Asia, near the larger countries of China and Japan. Korea is a **peninsula** south of China and west of Japan. The weather and land in Korea are very different in the far north than they are in the far south. But generally, winters are long and cold and summers are hot and wet.

In the Korean language, Korea is known as *Choson,* which means "land of morning calm."

*This is what a typical Korean village looked like when the first Korean **immigrants** came to the United States. Today, few buildings like this still exist in Korea.*

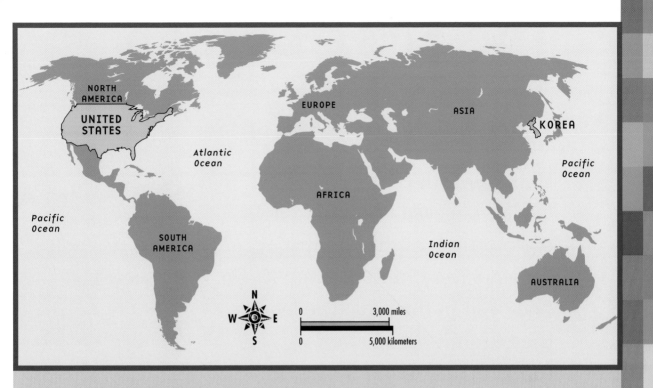

This map shows where Korea and the United States are located in the world.

Korea used to be one country. China, Russia, and Japan fought to gain control of Korea. Eventually, Japan won these conflicts. In 1905, Japan took control of Korea and held it until **World War Two.** The United States defeated Japan in that war in 1945. Today, Korea is divided into two countries. North Korea is a **communist** country that is about the size of the state of Mississippi. South Korea is a **republic** about the size of Indiana.

The First Korean Immigrants

Until the 19th century, Korean leaders believed they could hold on to control of the country by keeping everything the way it had been in the past. The leaders tried to shut out modern ways of thinking and doing things. In 1876, however, that changed.

Celebrations were held in May 2003 to remember some of the first Korean **immigrants** who came to Hawaii in 1903.

Japan had started selling goods to and buying goods from European countries. Japanese rulers pressured Korea to start doing the same.

These Korean men are wearing **traditional** *Korean clothes. They were representatives of Korea who lived in the United States and spoke for Korea in the late 1800s.*

These Korean women were part of a program in which they learned about medicine in the United States in the early 1900s.

In 1882, American **missionaries** began traveling to Korea to teach Koreans about **Christianity.** They also taught them about American ideas and **customs.** Some of the students became interested in learning more. Between 1890 and 1905, several dozen students came to the United States to study medicine and religion. Most of them returned to Korea when they finished school.

Coming to the United States

In the late 1800s and early 1900s, Hawaiian sugarcane farmers wanted people who would work hard for not much money. Many Chinese and Japanese people moved to Hawaii in the late 1800s to work. In the early 1900s, **plantation** owners tried to get new workers from Korea. In 1903, a **drought** hit Korea. Many people did not have enough food or money. Working in Hawaii sounded like a good idea.

In the early 1900s, Hawaii was an American **territory.** It did not officially become a state until 1959.

These Korean women and children lived in Hawaii in about 1910.

10

Korean men like these workers came to Hawaii from Korea to work in the sugarcane fields in the early 1900s.

Koreans were also unhappy about Japan controlling their country. They wanted to leave until Korea was **independent** again. Many of the people who wanted to leave did not have enough money to make the long trip. Plantation owners in Hawaii opened a bank in Korea that loaned Koreans the money they needed to travel. The people who took a loan then had to work on the plantations until the loan was repaid.

Life on the Plantations

Men and some women worked in the sugarcane fields for ten hours a day. They started working at five in the morning. Workers wore gloves, but they often finished the day with cuts on their hands from the sharp sugarcane leaves. They earned about $16 a week and had free places to live and medical care. Basic goods such as food and clothing cost the workers between $6 and $10 each week. It was difficult to save money to repay the loans.

This photo shows Korean men, women, and children who lived and worked on a plantation in Hawaii in the early 1900s.

These are the kinds of small houses that Korean immigrants lived in while they worked at the plantations.

Workers lived in camps on the **plantations.** Families were each given one small room to live in. Single men slept in buildings with many beds pushed together in each room. It was crowded and often dirty. Workers from China and Japan lived in separate camps. By keeping the groups separated, plantation owners kept workers from talking about how much they got paid. Each new group of **immigrants** might be paid less than those who were already working.

> Workers wore metal identification tags known as bangos. Each worker had a different bango number. The plantation owners called the workers by their numbers, not their names.

Life in the Cities and the Mainland

Most Koreans wanted to get off the **plantations** as quickly as possible. Many moved to Hilo and Honolulu, which were Hawaii's two largest cities. In the cities, they found work in factories that put pineapple in cans to sell in grocery stores. A few Koreans had been able to save enough money to start their own businesses, such as restaurants and grocery stores.

*Korean immigrants wanted their children to know about Korean **culture** and language. Korean schools, such as this one in Honolulu, were opened in the United States to teach Korean-American children about these things.*

Chun Duk Boo, a Korean-American business owner, is shown in front of his shoe-repair shop in San Francisco, California.

Many Korean **immigrants** moved to the **mainland.** They traveled across the Pacific Ocean to California. Most of them **settled** in California, but some went to Colorado and Alaska. The Koreans sometimes found it difficult to find work. Many people treated them unfairly just because they were from Korea and looked different. Koreans found ways to work together to start their own small farms and open their own businesses.

Korean immigrants would sometimes put their extra money into a kye, or a money-lending group. Each person would give money to the kye at a monthly meeting. Anyone who put money into the kye could borrow from it to start a new business.

War and Student Immigration

At the end of **World War Two** in 1945, the American defeat of Japan freed Korea from Japanese rule. In 1948, the country was officially divided. North Korea had a **communist** government. South Korea became a **republic.** In 1950, North Korea started trying to take control of South Korea, and the **Korean War** began. American soldiers were sent to South Korea to help fight against North Korea. The war lasted about three years. Many American soldiers married Korean women while they were in Korea.

When the Korean War ended, neither side had won. Today, Korea remains divided into two separate countries. More than 28,000 Korean wives of American soldiers moved to the United States from 1951 to 1964.

Peter Lee and his wife, shown standing, came to the U.S. from Korea as students in 1968. His children went on to become, from left to right, a businessperson, a banker, and a doctor.

After the war, a large number of Korean students came to the United States. Many of them **settled** in the United States and became scientists, doctors, professors, and lawyers. Today, many of the children of these students are doing the same types of jobs. Many Americans think of these people as community leaders.

Recent Korean Immigration

Early **immigration** laws in the United States kept the Korean population in the United States low. From 1900 to 1950, the number of Koreans living in the United States was never more than 10,000. The laws were changed in 1965 and 1968 to allow more immigrants from Korea. Today, about 35,000 Koreans move to the United States each year.

This map shows the states and cities that Koreans first came to and where many Korean Americans still live today.

Korean Immigration to the United States

United States

Largest Korean immigrant populations

400 kilometers

0   400 miles

Like this woman, many Koreans come to the United States to become doctors.

Some recent Korean immigrants are **refugees** from North Korea, but most come from South Korea. Most are well-educated people. Many Korean immigrants are doctors, nurses, and scientists. Some immigrants come to the United States to be with family members who are already American citizens. Others come because they want to work in the United States. They hope to be able to make more money than they could in Korea.

The largest wave of Korean immigration to date came between 1981 to 1990, when more than 300,000 Koreans moved to the United States.

Living and Working

Many Korean **immigrants** do not know how to speak English when they first arrive in the United States. This prevents some from finding well-paying jobs. Sometimes, immigrants work for Korean Americans who own their own businesses. This helps the immigrants save money and learn English. Korean Americans own many kinds of businesses including dry cleaners, fruit stands, and photo shops.

Sammy Lee, a Korean American, won gold medals in diving at the 1948 and 1952 Olympics. Lee was not only a talented athlete. He also did very well in school. Lee went to medical school and became a doctor.

This Korean-American family started their own business, as did many other Korean immigrants who came to the United States.

From 1965 to 1977, about 13,000 Korean doctors, nurses, **pharmacists**, and dentists came to the United States. Many came to finish their medical training and wanted to return to Korea. Others planned to stay in the United States. Those who had finished their training in Korea had to pass exams before they could work in the United States. The exams were written in English, so the immigrants had to be able to read and write English very well.

Celebrations

Many Korean Americans are **Christian.** They celebrate Christian holidays such as Christmas and Easter. Korean Americans also celebrate **Independence** Movement Day on March 1. On that day in 1919, many Koreans publicly spoke out against the Japanese people who were ruling Korea. The events marked the beginning of the Korean independence movement.

During *tol*, items are placed around the child. The item the child touches first has a meaning that tells something about the child.

Korean Americans have a special party for a child's first birthday, which is called *tol* in Korea. In earlier times in Korea, life was hard, and medicine was not always available.

The independence movement inspired many Korean-American artists, such as this dancer shown at a festival in Los Angeles.

*This Korean baby is shown celebrating his first birthday wearing a **traditional** Korean costume.*

Many children died before their first birthdays. A child's first birthday became a very important day. The family and community had a big party celebrating the baby's survival.

TOL ITEM	MEANING
bow and arrow	Child will be a strong fighter.
needle and thread	Child will have a long life.
jujube (chewy candy)	Child will have many children and grandchildren.
book or pencil	Child will be very successful in school.
rice	Child will become rich.
ruler, needle, or scissors	Child will be talented with his/her hands.
knife	Child will be a good cook.

Culture and Families

In recent years, many Korean **culture** schools have opened in the United States. Korean-American children can study Korean art, dance, language, and history. The schools are popular because Korean

Americans do not want their children to forget that they are not only American. They are Korean as well.

Our family goes to a Korean church so we are still in touch with our Korean culture. It's important to keep in touch with our culture and the church has been a big part of that.
—Younghee Hong, who came to the U.S. in 1989 at age 38

*In Los Angeles, these girls used fans to perform a **traditional** Korean dance.*

This American family from Wheaton, Illinois, adopted a girl from Korea. She attended grade school in Wheaton.

Americans adopted thousands of Korean children whose parents were killed in the **Korean War.** Americans continue to adopt Korean children today. Between 1978 and 1989, about 50,000 Korean **orphans** were adopted by Americans. Today, American parents of Korean children often make special efforts to have their children learn about Korea and Korean culture.

Korean Food

Korean food is similar to Japanese and Chinese food because rice is an ingredient in many dishes. Korean Americans also sometimes use chopsticks to eat instead of forks and knives, like Chinese and Japanese people do. Korean foods tend to be hot because spices such as garlic and red pepper are used in them. *Kong namul gook,* or soybean soup, and *bulgogi,* which is grilled beef, are popular Korean dishes.

These Korean-American people enjoyed a Korean meal in a restaurant in Los Angeles, California.

*Kimchi, shown above, is served at almost every Korean meal.
Many Korean Americans use chopsticks to eat their meals.*

Kimchi is usually part of a Korean meal. It is made up of cut-up cabbage, celery, turnips, and cucumbers. The vegetables are seasoned with red pepper, garlic, and onions and then put into large glass jars filled with salty water. The jars are then put underground in cellars or sheds for about a month. Shrimp and oysters are sometimes added for additional flavors.

Dr. John Han Today

John Han finished his medical training and became a doctor. He and his family moved to Woodstock, Illinois, in the 1970s.

Dr. Han's son, Patrick, and daughters, Wonson and Tanya, grew up as Korean Americans. John is happy that his children had the chance to get a good education in the United States. In Korea, children are expected to study very hard beginning at a very young age.

John and his wife sit on the couch together surrounded by their children and their children's families.

I never emphasized Korean **culture** with my children and now sometimes I regret it. But at that time, since we decided to stay in this country, I thought that teaching them to be American would be best for them.

—Dr. John Han

John is proud to be a Korean American. He has many American friends and interests, such as playing golf, but he always remembers he is Korean, too. Even though part of him wants to move back to Korea, he would not want to leave his friends and activities behind. John feels he is able to stay connected with his Korean roots by traveling to Korea once every two or three years. He visits friends, family, and some of his favorite places.

John travels to Korea to visit friends and family. He is on the left in this photo of him and his brothers and sisters-in-law in Korea.

29

Korean Immigration Chart

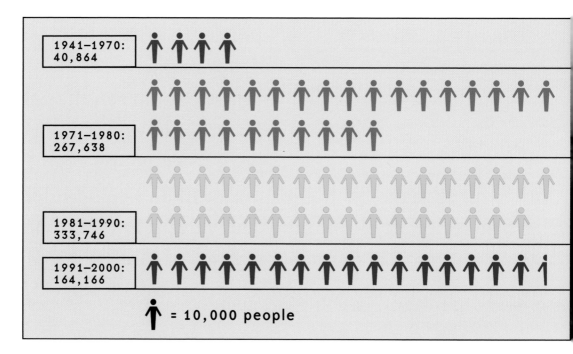

1941–1970: 40,864	🚶🚶🚶🚶
1971–1980: 267,638	🚶🚶🚶🚶🚶🚶🚶🚶🚶🚶🚶🚶🚶🚶🚶🚶🚶🚶 🚶🚶🚶🚶🚶🚶🚶🚶🚶
1981–1990: 333,746	🚶🚶🚶🚶🚶🚶🚶🚶🚶🚶🚶🚶🚶🚶🚶🚶🚶 🚶🚶🚶🚶🚶🚶🚶🚶🚶🚶🚶🚶🚶🚶🚶🚶
1991–2000: 164,166	🚶🚶🚶🚶🚶🚶🚶🚶🚶🚶🚶🚶🚶🚶🚶🚶

🚶 = 10,000 people

*The United States government did not start keeping track of Korean **immigrants** until 1948. But from 1948 to 2000, about 800,000 Korean people immigrated to the United States.*
Source: U.S. Immigration and Naturalization Service

More Books to Read

Burgan, Michael. *The Korean War.* Chicago: Heinemann Library, 2003.

Kim, Robert. *I Am Korean American.* New York: PowerKids Press, 1997.

Lee, O-Young. *Things Korean.* Rutland, Vt.: Charles E. Tuttle Company, 1999

Park, Linda Sue. *When My Name Was Keoko.* New York: Clarion Books, 2002.

Glossary

Christian someone who believes in Jesus and follows his teachings. The religion that Christians follow is called Christianity.

communist person or government that supports communism, a political system in which there is one party and government owns all factories and goods

culture ideas, skills, arts, and way of life for a group of people

custom way that people have done certain things for a long time

drought long period of time with little or no rain

immigrate to come to a country to live there for a long time. A person who immigrates is an immigrant.

independent condition of being free from the rule of other countries, governments, or people. The state of being independent is called independence.

Korean War war fought from 1950 to 1953 by North Korea and China on one side and South Korea and the United States on the other

mainland main part of a country, as opposed to island parts of a country

missionary person who goes to another country to teach people about religion

orphan child whose parents are dead. Sometimes, orphans live in places called orphanages.

peninsula strip of land that is surrounded by water on three sides

pharmacist person who prepares and sells drugs and medicine according to a doctor's orders

plantation large farm where crops are grown by workers who live there

refugee person who leaves his or her native country to escape war or danger

republic country in which people vote to elect their leaders

retired no longer working a job, usually because of old age

settle to make a home for yourself and others

territory large division or area of a nation. People who live in a territory have some but not all of the same rights.

tradition belief or practice handed down through the years from one generation to the next

World War Two war fought from 1939 to 1945 by Germany, Japan, and Italy on one side and the United States, Great Britain, China, Poland, France, and the Soviet Union on the other

Index